Genre Folktale

Essential Question
How can we understand nature?

How
Turtles
Found Their
Homes

Cast of Characters

TURTLE   MONKEY

ELEPHANT   MOUSE

PARROT   HIPPO

Scene 1
Turtle Needs a Home

Setting: A rainforest in West Africa

TURTLE: This forest looks like a beautiful home for my children. *(to Elephant)* Is this a good place to live?

ELEPHANT: Only fast or strong animals can live here. I am both. You look slow and weak. This is not a good place for you to live.

TURTLE: *(to himself)* Elephant is too proud. We have more similarities than she thinks. *(to Elephant)* I don't like to boast. But I can prove that I am fast and strong. Let's have a tug-of-war.

2

Parrot

Monkey

forest

Elephant

Turtle

Mouse

PARROT: *(surprised)* Turtle asked Elephant to have a tug-of-war!

MONKEY: *(hooting)* We will get plenty of laughs!

MOUSE: You should be ashamed, Monkey. It's not nice to <u>make fun of others</u>. Elephant will give Turtle a chance to prove how strong he is.

In Other Words   tease. En español: reírse de.

3

ELEPHANT: *(unhappy)* If I must.
But it won't take me long to win.
We can use my rope.

TURTLE: *(taking one end of the rope)*
I will sit in the river. If you can pull me out,
you win. If I stay in the river, I win.

ELEPHANT: No problem. I will go
into the forest.

TURTLE: Holler when you are ready.

rope

river

PARROT: I want to go with Elephant!

MONKEY: Me, too!

MOUSE: Wait for me!

STOP AND CHECK

Why is there a tug-of-war?

5

Scene 2
Tugging From the River

TURTLE: I need to move fast. *(diving underwater)* I will tie my end of the rope around this big rock. Elephant can never pull it out.

ELEPHANT: *(hollering)* I'm ready!

TURTLE: *(sitting in the river again)* Me, too! *(to himself)* They don't know that I'm pulling the middle of the rope!

PARROT: Elephant is losing!
I am going to dash back
and watch Turtle win!

MONKEY: Me, too!

MOUSE: Wait for me!

PARROT: *(pointing at Turtle)*
Look how strong Turtle is!

MONKEY: *(laughing)* This is funny!

MOUSE: Here comes
Elephant! She lost!

STOP AND CHECK

What did Turtle
do with his rope?

ALL: Three cheers
for Turtle's victory!

8

Scene 3

Tugging From the Land

TURTLE: Stop, you are embarrassing me!
(diving underwater to untie the rope)

HIPPO: *(swimming by)* It's too loud here!

TURTLE: *(appearing again with rope)* Sorry.
We were having a tug-of-war.

PARROT: Turtle beat Elephant!
Turtle is the strongest animal
in the forest!

Hippo

HIPPO: Turtle is not stronger than me. I will <u>have</u> a tug-of-war with Turtle! I will pull from the river. Turtle will pull from land. If Turtle pulls me out of the river, he wins. If I pull him into the river, I win.

TURTLE: Okay.

tree

land

Language Detective

<u>Have</u> is a helping verb. Find another helping verb on the page.

PARROT: I'm going to stay here with Hippo. He is the strongest animal in the forest!

MONKEY: Yes. I'll sit near Hippo and watch.

MOUSE: Me, too.

ELEPHANT: I'm too tired to move!

TURTLE: *(hiding behind a tree)* I will tie the rope around this big tree. Hippo cannot pull me into the river. *(hollering)* I'm ready!

HIPPO: *(hollering)* Me, too!

PARROT: Oh, no!

MONKEY: Hippo is <u>having trouble</u>.

MOUSE: Hippo will lose!

ELEPHANT: Turtle seems strong.

In Other Words struggling.
En español: tiene problemas.

HIPPO: I can't pull anymore.

PARROT: Hippo lost!

MONKEY: I can't believe it!

ELEPHANT: Turtle *is* strong!

TURTLE: *(untying the rope)*
I did it! *(calling)*
I'll be right there!

STOP AND CHECK

Why did
Hippo lose?

Scene 4

Home Sweet Homes

ELEPHANT: *(to Turtle)* You beat me very fast. You can live in the forest.

HIPPO: You can live in the river, too. I need a strong friend like you!

TURTLE: My family is happy to have two homes. Some turtles will live on land. Some turtles will live in water. It is good to be fast and strong! *(to himself)* But it is better to have wisdom!

Respond to Reading

Summarize

Use important details to summarize *How Turtles Found Their Homes.*

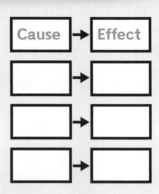

Text Evidence

1. How do you know *How Turtles Found Their Homes* is a folktale? Genre

2. How does Turtle get to live in the forest and in the river? Cause and Effect

3. What is the root word in *embarrassing* on page 9? Root Words

4. How do you feel about how Turtle wins tug-of-war? Write a sentence. Write About Reading

Compare Texts

Read a folktale about a pine tree.

Why Pine Trees Have Green Needles

Illustrated by Amanda Hall

A little Pine Tree was in the forest. He was sad. "The other trees look beautiful. I look boring."

A girl with gold bracelets came by. "I wish my needles were gold," said Pine Tree. Then his needles turned gold! Soon, two men came and picked the needles to sell.

The next day, Little Pine Tree heard the sweet sound of a glass wind chime. "I wish I had needles like that," he said. Then his needles were glass! But soon, a strong wind blew and the needles broke.

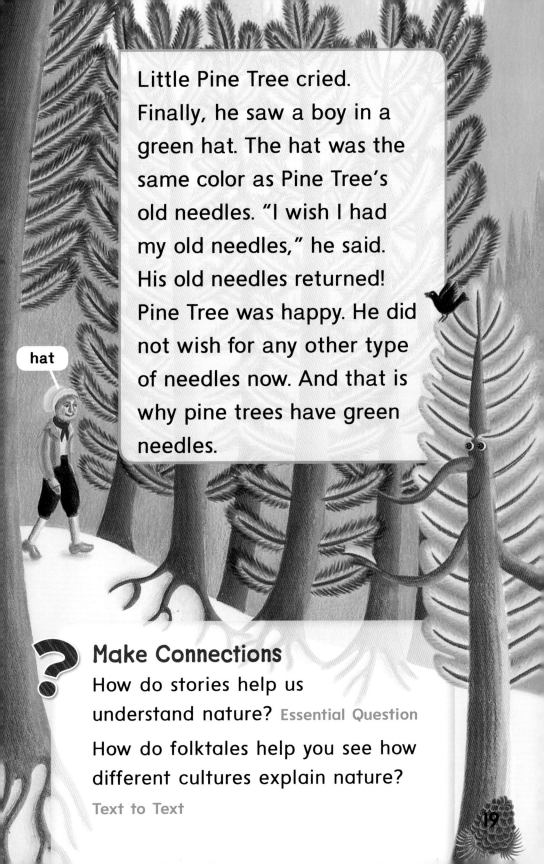

Little Pine Tree cried. Finally, he saw a boy in a green hat. The hat was the same color as Pine Tree's old needles. "I wish I had my old needles," he said. His old needles returned! Pine Tree was happy. He did not wish for any other type of needles now. And that is why pine trees have green needles.

hat

? Make Connections

How do stories help us understand nature? **Essential Question**

How do folktales help you see how different cultures explain nature?

Text to Text

19

Focus on
Literary Elements

Theme The theme is the message in a story or drama.

What to Look for Look at what the other animals say about Turtle. Notice why they change their opinions.

Your Turn

Plan a folktale drama about nature. What is the message of your drama? What part of nature will you explain? Think about what your characters will do. Write your ideas. Share them with a partner.

favorite character? Why?